6-99

BFI FILM CLASSICS

· ·

Edward Buscombe
SERIES EDITOR

Colin MacCabe and David Meeker
SERIES CONSULTANTS

Cinema is a fragile medium. Many of the great classic films of the past now exist, if at all, in damaged or incomplete prints. Concerned about the deterioration in the physical state of our film heritage, the National Film and Television Archive, a Division of the British Film Institute, has compiled a list of 360 key films in the history of the cinema. The long-term goal of the Archive is to build a collection of perfect show-prints of these films, which will then be screened regularly at the Museum of the Moving Image in London in a year-round repertory.

BFI Film Classics is a series of books commissioned to stand alongside these titles. Authors, including film critics and scholars, film-makers, novelists, historians and those distinguished in the arts, have been invited to write on a film of their choice, drawn from the Archive's list. Each volume presents the author's own insights into the chosen film, together with a brief production history and a detailed filmography, notes and bibliography. The numerous illustrations have been specially made from the Archive's own prints.

With new titles published each year, the BFI Film Classics series will rapidly grow into an authoritative and highly readable guide to the great films of world cinema.

Could scarcely be improved upon ... informative, intelligent, jargon-free companions.
The Observer

Cannily but elegantly packa̶ ̶ ̶ ̶ ̶ ̶ ̶ ̶ ̶ ̶ at   75075
addition to the most discerni
New Statesman & Society

D1471858

084539

BFI FILM CLASSICS

ODD MAN OUT

·····················

Dai Vaughan

BRITISH FILM INSTITUTE

bfi

BFI PUBLISHING

First published in 1995 by the
BRITISH FILM INSTITUTE
21 Stephen Street, London WIP 2LN

Copyright © Dai Vaughan 1995

The British Film Institute exists
to promote appreciation, enjoyment, protection and
development of moving image culture in and throughout
the whole of the United Kingdom.
Its activities include the National Film and
Television Archive; the National Film Theatre;
the Museum of the Moving Image,
the London Film Festival; the production and
distribution of film and video; funding and support for
regional activities; Library and Information Services;
Stills, Posters and Designs; Research,
Publishing and Education; and the monthly
Sight and Sound magazine.

ST. HELENS
COLLEGE

791 · 43 72

84539

NOV 1996

LIBRARY

British Library Cataloguing-in-Publication Data
A catalogue record for this book is available from the British Library

ISBN 0-85170-493-X

Stills courtesy of Rank Film Distributors Ltd.

Designed by
Andrew Barron & Collis Clements Associates

Typesetting by
Fakenham Photosetting Limited, Fakenham, Norfolk

Printed in Great Britain by
The Trinity Press, Worcester

CONTENTS

. . . .

Metaphysical rebellion is the justified claim of a desire for unity against the suffering of life and death – in that it protests against the incompleteness of life, expressed by death, and its dispersion, expressed by evil.

Albert Camus, The Rebel

Social values are rules of conduct implicit in a tragic fate; and they offer a hope of creation.

Herbert Read, foreword to The Rebel[1]

ACKNOWLEDGMENT

I owe a debt of gratitude to John Huntley, who first excited my interest in this film with his BFI evening lectures in 1955–6.

Production still of James Mason

FOREWORD

. . . .

It is a little surprising, when you think about it, how many fiction films have relied for their narrative resolution upon the elimination of a central character by gunshot. Faced with the killing which brings *Odd Man Out* to an end, one may call to mind any number of parallels: for instance, that of Cagney on the church steps in *The Roaring Twenties*, with which it shares an iconography of religion and snow. The device was to appear with considerable baroque elaboration in Wajda's *Ashes and Diamonds* and again, heavily clad in quotation marks, in Godard's *A Bout de souffle*. James Mason, who plays the leading role of Johnny in *Odd Man Out*, provides in his autobiography a list of deaths undergone in a succession of twenty-nine movies up to 1954, thirteen of them by small arms fire.[2]

Statistics are lacking, but it seems a safe bet that the proportion of such endings is higher for cinema than for literature; and I suspect that this has to do less with box-office demands for sensation than with inherent differences between film and writing as narrative media. With writing it is possible, and not at all unusual, to begin with the mind of an individual and to present the objective world, as and when necessary, as what is available to that mind. With film, although characters and their lines of vision offer the readiest means for articulating space, the characters are themselves presented always as inseparable from a context, as part of an image: so that while there may at a pinch be locations without persons, there can be no persons without locations. Thus, since the place occupied by a character remains unchanged when that character has gone, death in film – especially when it is sudden – offers a more tersely inevitable sense of bereavement. It is the very space before us that is bereft of a potential point of vantage.

I shall return to such questions later; and it will be my suggestion that the view of life proposed by *Odd Man Out* is one which emerges with particular cogency through properties specific to the medium.

. . . .

'Mason Back – In the Best Film of All Time.' That was the headline of Paul Dehn's review in the *Sunday Chronicle* of 2 February 1947, greeting *Odd Man Out* on its first release. 'It is more than a milestone', he stated.

'It is a terminus.' While other critics did not go quite so far in their praise, their response was generally very favourable; and many seemed to feel this was the best film yet made in Britain. A few small reservations were voiced by some – indeed, by Dehn himself. These mainly concerned the performance of Robert Newton as a demented artist, the use of optical 'tricks' to represent Mason's delirium, and the fact that a story ostensibly about an IRA action had seemingly been drained of political content.

Serious dissent came from a surprising quarter. *Documentary News Letter*, launched at the beginning of the war, had begun in 1945 to carry anonymous reviews of prominent fiction films. In the issue for April/ May 1947, editors Edgar Anstey and Basil Wright announced that they had differed so fundamentally in their opinions of *Odd Man Out* as to be unable to maintain the convention of editorial unanimity. Instead, the journal printed a substantial review by each of them – to be followed, in a later issue, by a letter disagreeing vehemently with both.

Anstey, having begun by assuring us that he does not visit the cinema purely in pursuit of social significance, launches into:

> ... but I cannot escape the conclusion that *Odd Man Out* is a shocking film. Not so much in content or in manner as in the fact that it has been made at all. And then again less shocking in its making than in the eulogies with which it has been received. ... Cast your mind back to Germany after the last war [i.e. 1914–18]. In those days the morbid screen drama of the helpless individual struggling against malignant circumstances was high art. ... But later it became clear that the mood which they represented, and indeed fortified, provided an ideal springboard for coming totalitarian theories. ... Let us watch carefully to see that in periods of cold, discouraging weather we do not too readily accept the view that the defeat of all humanity's aspirations is not only inevitable but aesthetically admirable.

Why, one must ask, did a fiction film provoke such outrage in a magazine devoted nominally to documentary? There are several points to be taken into account. First: the documentary movement always made the assumption that what was done in films had consequences in the real world. Second: during the war, documentarists had begun making feature-length, narrative movies at the same time as commercial film-making had been edging towards greater realism; and many documentarists still hoped that such infiltration of the cinemas by actuality might continue into the postwar period. And third: this was a time when people believed, in a manner scarcely imaginable today, that a betterment of the human condition was possible through political means. Setting aside the somewhat tendentious comparison with German cinema of the 1930s, I think it is worth keeping Anstey's reaction in the back of our mind as we look more closely at *Odd Man Out*, not so much to judge him right or wrong as to identify what it was about the film that so upset him.

When set against Anstey's attack, Wright's defence seems a trifle woolly. He is reduced to generalisations about the film's stature as a work of art, and to such vague specifics as, 'The little girl with one roller skate is in my opinion one of the loveliest images in movies since the dancing peasant in Dovzhenko's *Earth*.' But this problem he shares with nearly all the critics, who, having noted the subtlety of the soundtrack or the brilliance of the performances or the sensitivity of the direction, are left saying little more than that it is a great film because it moved them emotionally, and that it moved them emotionally because it is a great film.

If that sounds like a sneer, it is not meant to be. The difficulties are genuine. Nothing we can say about a film can *prove* that it is any good – or that it isn't. The assertion of quality demands an act of judgment, of investment of the self. As with any other work of art, there is an unbridgeable gap between its objective properties, which may be measured and enumerated, dissected to the last tremor, and the value placed upon them, the significance inferred into them, by the intuitive and constructive grasp of the individual. Reviewers usually deal with this by smuggling in their value judgments, adjectivally as it were, along with their descriptions: the discreet camera movement, the well-observed detail, the splendid climax. ... Academic writers more frequently pretend that their judgment is not in play at all, and will analyse the symbolic interactions of a work as if signs held parley among themselves and required no subjective consciousness for their translation into meaning. (In this sense, academic criticism exemplifies the much reviled 'classic realist text', concealing the evidence of its own production.) The most we can do – and here, obviously, I must set out my own stall – is to account as honestly as possible for the experience which we as individuals have taken from a film, and to do so by reference to what is actually there on the screen. We are not required to show, or even to believe, that the significances we find were necessarily those intended by the film-makers. What matters is that they should be integral to the film's coherence. Of course, the act of analysis may itself lead us to modify our initial impressions; but there is no harm in that. Analysis, too, is part of life.

However, in case we should begin to think the alignment of opinions a simple thing, let me offer, as an example of the way an argument can turn on its axis to reveal another face, Carol Reed's comment on the so-called 'kitchen sink' films of the early 60s:

> I believe that this tendency is passing quickly because the public go to the cinema to get away from the dirt and depression which are caused by their own problems. It is not reasonable to take people to see a film which stresses their own unhappiness. Such people should be given optimism, happiness and hope.[3]

The key to any apparent contradiction in Reed's attitude here may lie in the fact that he was a director who showed little inclination ever to rebel against popular taste; and he seems to have believed in 1945 that the war, with its mixed diet of escapism and propaganda, had left people with an appetite for 'serious' cinema.

Reed himself was at this time thirty-eight years of age and at the peak of his promise. A string of sixteen productions over nine years – including *Bank Holiday* (1938), *The Stars Look Down* (1940) and *The Way Ahead* (1944), and culminating in the feature-length documentary of the progress from D-Day to the Allied victory in Europe, *The True Glory* (1945) – had left him free of contractual shackles and free, for the first time, to choose his own subject with the confidence of being able to raise finance purely on the strength of his reputation. He read F. L. Green's novel *Odd Man Out* shortly after it was published, and took out an immediate option on it.[4]

Yet despite the success of this venture, Reed's now commanding status did not lead him to the development of an individualised manner of the kind congenial to the theories of the critical establishment; and this was almost certainly a consequence of his perception of the director

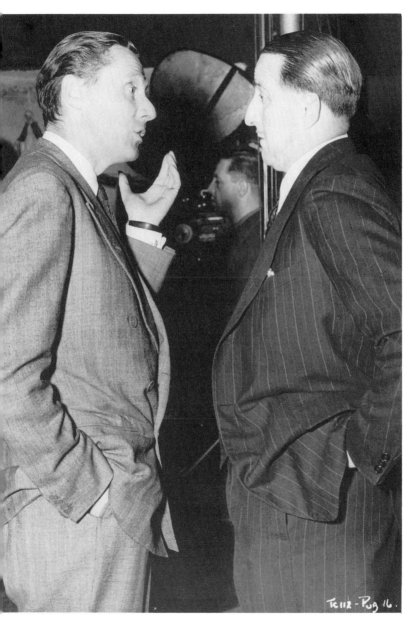

TC 118 - Pag 16.

Carol Reed (l.) with J. Arthur Rank

1 3

as someone skilled in a craft, supplying a service, and of his pride in his ability to turn his hand to any style or genre. One response would be to ask whether someone who has made one great film and half a dozen very good ones truly merits the critical neglect to which Reed has been subjected. Another would be to ask whether a great film necessarily presupposes a great director.

1

. . . .

The main title and opening credits are superimposed upon a rough drawing of docklands. We then mix to an aerial shot approaching an urban area, over which a roller-title informs us, *inter alia*, that the story 'is told against a background of political unrest in a city of Northern Ireland'. This sentence has attracted some comment, since the title has no sooner faded than we mix to another aerial shot, moving in towards the clock-tower of what, to anyone who knows it, is clearly Belfast. Why then not say so? One possibility is that this is just a hangover from the wartime habit of never admitting where anywhere was; another is

A street of terraced dwellings

that it is meant for overseas audiences for whom 'Belfast' might not be a significant place-name; but a third, perhaps more interesting, is that it is saying to us, 'Although we have shot much of this film in recognisable locations, we want you to see them as contributing only to a notional city' – in other words, asserting a subtle discrimination between reading for fiction and for fact.

From a low-angle shot of the clock-tower we tilt down and track right, taking in as we do so a gang of noisy boys running towards the open dock gates in the background, to find Dennis (Robert Beatty) browsing at a bookstall; and as the clock strikes four, he purposefully puts down the book and moves off. He approaches along a street of terraced dwellings, a little girl idling in a doorway, an unseen baby crying – children being urged upon our attention – and crosses the road to enter the house where Granny (Kitty Kirwan) is waiting for him. As he goes up the stairs, we mix quickly into the bedroom; and as he enters, we pan with him across a cluster of people to where Johnny (James Mason) is seated on the bed giving final instructions for a raid. Since there is no significant telescoping of time between the staircase shot and the one inside the bedroom, it is hard to see why a dissolve

Production still of Kathleen (Kathleen Ryan) and Johnny (James Mason)

was used here rather than a cut. Perhaps its function is to accustom the viewer as early as possible to a certain fluidity in the handling of spatial and temporal transitions: a fluidity which will, however, be held in discipline by the successive chiming and striking of the city clock.

This opening scene is packed with information, and introduces in short order no fewer than eight significant characters. Present in the room to begin with are the three men who will accompany Johnny on the raid – Pat (Cyril Cusack), Nolan (Dan O'Herlihy) and Murphy (Roy Irving) – as well as a young woman called Kathleen (Kathleen Ryan). There is an odd moment during this phase of the exposition. Pat is balancing a small teddy bear on his knee, and Kathleen draws attention to it by picking it up, looking at it, then giving it back to him. We know that, in the normal context of a thriller, such a gesture signifies that the object in question will later take on narrative importance. But it does not; and we forget it. Why then is it there? Is it to signify that Pat is of a childish disposition? He is nervy and impulsive, arguably unreliable, and will certainly make serious errors of judgment; but 'childish' is not, I think, a word one would apply to him. Perhaps the teddy bear is there for no other reason than to keep the undercurrent of childhood running quietly through this otherwise all-adult portion of the film.

We hear the city clock chime the quarter; and Johnny remarks that there is time for a cup of tea before they leave. Kathleen goes downstairs. A brief exchange with Granny establishes that she is in love with Johnny. Then Maureen – the last of the eight characters – arrives and, after some talk with Granny about food coupons, goes up to join the others. It will be Maureen's task to spirit away the money they are to steal; and some of it will be allocated to helping her while her husband is in prison. 'A slice of the party cake,' Nolan says to her. (It is the only reference to a 'party'; otherwise, what we assume to be the IRA will be referred to, throughout, simply as the 'Organisation'.) Then all leave to take up their positions except Johnny, Dennis and Kathleen; and a conversation follows in which first Dennis, then later Kathleen, try to persuade Johnny that he is not in a fit condition to lead the robbery, and that he should let Dennis go instead. In this context we learn that Johnny has served eight months of a seventeen-year sentence for importing arms, and has been hidden in the house for the six months since his escape. But Johnny will have none of it. 'I'm the leader of the

Organisation in this city. ... I've got my orders, and I'll see them through.'

Embedded here is a key exchange where Dennis suggests to Johnny that his heart is not in the raid. He replies that 'this violence isn't getting us anywhere'. He observes, 'In prison you have time to think', and expresses the wish – not necessarily the belief, but the wish – that they could throw their guns away and make their cause in the parliaments. If *Odd Man Out* were about the politics of Northern Ireland, the arguments would have had to be developed beyond that. The fact that it is not is a clear indication that the film – made during a period of quiescence in IRA activity – is about other things altogether. What this exchange really does is to help establish Johnny as someone who has lost all taste for killing. It is worth noting, in this connection, that the only specific use mentioned for the stolen money is to help Maureen and, by implication, others fallen on hard times.

Obviously the question of Johnny's culpability cannot entirely be dissociated – as will be made even more obvious by later events – from that of his physical and psychological fitness for the task in hand. From the very beginning of the scene, before anything has been said on such matters, we are aware that there is something unsettling, something *wrong* about it. Johnny's voice is gentle, almost weak, inappropriate to the content of what he is saying and to the orders he is giving. Perhaps, if his voice were firmer, Pat could not credibly be seen playing with the teddy bear. The way Johnny is seated on the bed has connotations of prison; but perhaps, more significantly, of someone being visited by relatives in hospital. His eyes are at moments over-bright, consumptive, girlish. As he reassures Kathleen that 'It'll go fine', he breaks a shoelace – a piece of symbolism which may seem a little heavy-handed in itself but will have its justification in due course. But don't we know too, from our experience of the movies, if not from common sense, that it is unwise for a wanted man to sit at an open and uncurtained window? We tend to see this film as following a trajectory from realism to expressionism; but the expressionism is there from the start.

. . . .

As Pat drives the four of them to the mill where the robbery is to take place, Johnny is assaulted by a barrage of images – buses, buildings, wheels, tramlines, pedestrians –which he can hardly assemble into a

coherent meaning. Things are happening too quickly. The light is hurting his eyes, and the focus blurs. They reach the front steps of the mill, and Johnny alights with Nolan and Murphy. He glances up, and we see a huge smoke-stack towering above him. (Some people, I suppose, might register this as premonitory of a smoking gun; and I have no grounds for arguing that they would be mistaken.)

Johnny pulls himself together, and the three of them enter the building and walk with their briefcases – pretending to be businessmen – to the administrative area, where the safe is already open and the money being counted. The robbery is rendered with a light touch – no unpleasantness. But while it is going on, we find Pat becoming anxious as a horse-drawn coal cart moves slowly forward and threatens to block the route of their escape. As the three leave with their briefcases full of banknotes, the alarm bell rings. They break into a run; and as Johnny emerges through the swing doors he is hit by the full glare of the light. His foot hesitates on the top step. A man with a gun comes out to challenge him; they grapple, fall and roll down the steps. The man shoots Johnny in the shoulder; and Johnny, trying to break free, turns his own gun towards him. The actual shot occurs over a cutaway of Murphy and Nolan coming back to help. They try to drag Johnny into the car as Pat, afraid of the escape gap closing, accelerates off.

The killing on the steps can hardly fail to remind us of another murder occasioned by lassitude, sunlight and a real or imagined threat: that of the Arab by Meursault in Camus's *L'Étranger*.[5] Meursault's sensitivity to light and heat has been carefully pre-established in a way that recalls the neurasthenic quality of the opening scenes of *Odd Man Out*; and Johnny's moral uncertainties find a parallel in the refusal of Meursault to live according to the prescriptions of those around him. (For Meursault, to fall in with the expectations of others is simply bad faith. But by stripping away such bad faith Camus arrives, as a sort of philosophical desideratum, at something very close to that form of 'high-functioning' autism known as Asperger's syndrome: a lack of intuitive apprehension for others' subjectivity.[6]) In both cases, the question of guilt has been made to vanish into near-irrelevancy. It remains to be seen whether this comparison will prove of any further help to us.

. . . .

Murphy and Nolan struggle to pull Johnny into the car, but as Pat takes a sharp corner they lose their grip and he falls out. Pat stops the car some way further on; and while they are all arguing about whether to back the car up or to get out and fetch him, Johnny rises and runs off in the wrong direction, down a side street, chased by a dog. The others try to head him off at the next corner, but he is nowhere to be seen – only a vista of street-level air-raid shelters and children playing. The men decide to go back to Kathleen's and hope that Johnny will find his own way there. Then we cut to a couple of high-angle shots of Johnny, still chased by the dog, running across some waste ground. He finally reaches the safety of one of the shelters, where he sinks to the floor. The music, which has accompanied the getaway, fades out; and we realise that the alarm bell of the mill is still distantly audible. The camera pans down to Johnny's hand as blood trickles down his sleeve.[7]

From this hand there is a quick mix to the hand of a policeman swinging up to halt a car. And music begins again to accompany a montage of the police demanding people's identity cards. It is a device used several times in this film, the reintroduction of music very soon after a previous music section has finished; and it helps to create an agitation in which we feel no respite can last long. The montage ends with a hand drawing a line on a map to enclose the city. The music ceases, and we are with a rabble of children taunting the police as they come and go from a station across the road.

Children have been in evidence from the very start of *Odd Man Out*; and it is clear by now that they are not there simply to add verisimilitude to the street scenes. What is their function? Films featuring children were enjoying something of a vogue in Europe at the end of the war. Examples which spring to mind are Rossellini's *Germania anno zero* (1948), Clément's *Jeux interdits* (1952), even Crichton's Ealing comedy *Hue and Cry* (1947). The feeling that adults had made a mess of the world, and that the young had the right to judge their moral behaviour harshly, is aptly summed up in the title of De Sica's *I bambini ci guardano* (*The Children are Watching Us* [1943]). Then again, Carol Reed had a particular penchant for the child's-eye view, and was to explore it further in *The Fallen Idol*, *A Kid for Two Farthings* and *Oliver!* But in *Odd Man Out* one feels that something more specific is at work. These children are a constant but shifting presence, sometimes intersecting with the action, sometimes mocking it, more often seeming unaware of it in pursuit of their own purposes. They have no principles and no loyalties. They parody adult categories. They are on nobody's side. 'Could I have the thousand pound reward if I catch Johnny?' shouts one, laughing; and a smiling, grubby *putto* adds, 'Alive or dead!' It seems wholly appropriate that a child should be the first to mention the reward; though their information, as we shall see, is not always trustworthy. They are an anarchic, inchoate, corrosive substratum of the city's consciousness. To imagine the film without them is to imagine something thinner, more purely expository, less bonded. As more police emerge from the station and down its steps, one child runs towards them with a wooden gun, shouting, 'I'm Johnny McQueen, I'm Johnny McQueen, all police are looking for me...' – and then they scatter.

Next there is a little gem of a scene in Granny's kitchen, done almost in one take, where Pat is giving Dennis his account of what went wrong at the mill when Nolan and Murphy arrive to offer their conflicting versions. No one is exactly lying, yet the stories do not add up. Maureen enters as this is going on, and expresses her contempt for all three of them. Since they have only just got back, having presumably

'a rabble of children taunting the police'

disposed of the car, the scene serves retrospectively to tell us how quickly news of the raid has spread among the children.

In the shelter, off-screen children's voices rouse Johnny. Football is being played on a bomb-site. A little girl with one roller-skate chases after the ball as it is kicked out of play; and a passer-by skies it so that it lands on top of the shelter, bounces and rolls in. Johnny turns at the sound. Prison bars dissolve over the doorway, and a warder comes in to retrieve the ball. Johnny starts to tell him of a dream he has had, and recounts the story of the raid on the mill. The warder stands immobile and impassive, as if cut out of cardboard. As Johnny reaches the part where he arrives, wounded, in an air-raid shelter, he becomes aware of his surroundings; and the warder dissolves into the little girl, who hurriedly leaves. This is a sequence which might seem a little stale were there not a certain ambiguity in it: a discomfort just below the surface. We have all encountered the filmic device where something presented in fully concrete terms is revealed to have been 'only a dream'; and while there is little likelihood that we will imagine this is to be the case here, and that Johnny will turn out never to have left the prison, it is a fact that the lucidity of Johnny's speech contradicts the degree of delirium implied in his hallucination of the warder. Are we to assume, then, that this lucidity is itself illusory, a part of the dream-of-having-dreamt, and that the image we see of Johnny is therefore his own image of himself – rather than, say, the little girl's? This may seem a small point, but it contributes to a cumulative unease in the representation of Johnny of which we have had hints already and which will, I think, become more marked as the film progresses. It certainly adds to the frisson of the moment when he returns to consciousness.

....

Darkness has fallen. In the kitchen, with the others still present, Dennis is finishing writing his report. The evening paper carries the news: 'Armed raid on mill. Cashier killed in desperate struggle. Wounded assailant still at large.' Maureen says, 'Poor Johnny – may heaven protect him!' and she goes out into the night with the money. Dennis instructs the three men to return to headquarters, and says he is going out to look for Johnny. He asks Kathleen to bandage his arm in case he needs to act as a decoy for the police, who know Johnny is wounded. As she does so, she asks if she can go with him.

'Why?'

'Something I want to do.'

'Something you want to do for yourself, and not the Organisation.'

As he departs, having ordered her to stay behind, we mix out from Kathleen, seated at a table, to a street scene. But it is worth noticing that the final shot of Kathleen is not simply a static hold. At the very moment of the dissolve – cueing it, in fact – she begins to get up. Is she about to disobey Dennis? We do not know. But in any case, action is felt to be continuing without us. It is details such as this that give the film its sense of fullness as well as its urgency.

Pat, Nolan and Murphy find themselves trapped between groups of police checking people's papers. At one moment, in an attempt to behave innocently, they pause and gaze into a shop window which – though the point is so understated as almost to pass unnoticed – is completely empty. They finally make a dash for it, and there is a chase in which they throw off their pursuers. Pat insists that it is too dangerous to try to reach headquarters at present, and that they should make for 'Theresa's house' and wait there until the streets are clear. At the very door Murphy, saying he does not trust Theresa, sets off for his mother's. The other two go in. Theresa (Maureen Delaney), having deftly drawn a curtain to conceal what is evidently an illicit card game, takes their coats; then, responding to the weight of the guns in their pocket, she says, 'For your own peace of mind, now, you'd better keep these handy' – and gives them back. 'Come on into the warm and rest yourselves.'

In a complex play of oppositions, we return to the miserable refuge of the shelter where Johnny is divesting himself of his shoulder-holster. He begins to shuffle towards the door; but as he does so, we cut to a young man entering; and Johnny is seen backing again into the shadow. A young woman enters hesitantly to sit beside the man, and a sad little attempt at seduction ensues:

'What's wrong?'

'I don't want to.'

'You said you would.'

'Yes, I know; but I've changed my mind. Anyway, Lennie, I've got a stye.'

The sheer banality of it stands in touching contrast with Johnny's predicament. Then a slight movement on his part attracts their attention, and the man comes forward and lights a match. Summoning an authority greater than he has displayed at any point in the film, Johnny snaps: 'Put it out! Clear off!' The young man lets the match fall. 'It's that fella – Johnny.' As the two of them scuttle away, Johnny moves to the entrance and looks out. Children in an alley are playing hopscotch. He collapses to the ground again.

A bridging shot of Dennis looking around deserted streets takes us back to Theresa's. Nolan and Pat, clearly the worse for drink, are telling the whole story of the raid to Theresa, who sits between them refilling their glasses. Though maintaining the residue of what we imagine to be her normal fake-motherly manner, she is now scarcely bothering to conceal her lust for information; and as we watch, she elicits the fact that Dennis is out looking for Johnny, and that their centre of operations has been Kathleen's house. She rises from the arm of Pat's chair, adjusting her corsets from behind – a piece of social observation that will be lost on younger audiences – and turns on the radio; and, to the strains of Schubert's 8th symphony, she gestures to the card-players to leave as she goes into the telephone cubicle to contact the police. Pat and Nolan now begin to doubt the wisdom of having told Theresa so much; but her food, whisky and cigarettes remain foremost in their minds. This drunken scene between them – though perfectly gauged, never played for caricature – has moments of Chaplinesque humour from Cusack which most film-makers might have discouraged at such a point in the drama. But it was always characteristic of Carol Reed to be willing, in almost Shakespearean fashion, to throw in a joke at a moment of high seriousness.

Theresa reappears and announces that the police have phoned to say they are on their way round. She hustles Pat and Nolan out of the door – 'There are three steps' – and shuts it behind them. They emerge to challenge the police who, except for one shadow, remain unseen. Can they really have arrived so quickly, or is this just a drunken panic? Over a close-up of Theresa listening at the door, we hear shots and an answering fusillade; and we cut to two bodies lying on the steps: another outcome of the struggle on the steps of the mill. We pan up as someone enters. A policeman? No, a child, who is arriving with his mother and brother just as Theresa emerges from the house. The city clock is striking seven; but there is so much happening at once that you could hardly be expected to register that. The police arrive at this point, and the Inspector (Denis O'Dea), with noticeable lack of sympathy, takes Theresa inside to talk to her.

. . . .

Police cars are speeding past. Dennis is taking cover. He runs off down a now familiar alley: one of those disquieting shots in which the shadow seems to grow larger as he diminishes, contradicting and cancelling the sense of his movement. A surge of off-screen children's voices heralds another re-enactment, on tenement steps, of the events at the mill: 'Go on, Johnny, shoot him.' In this version Johnny and the cashier, both seemingly dead, are tended by their respective supporters. Then Dennis enters, and the children crowd around him begging for money. He questions them about the movements of the police and the whereabouts of Johnny, but begins to lose interest as he realises they really know nothing. At the same time, however, he becomes aware of the little girl standing by a lamp-post across the road. The first time we cut to her, in long-shot, it is almost casual – scarcely demanded at all by his glance: as if *she* were somehow calling *him* into the orbit of significance, rather than the reverse. The second time, his look cues a conventional mid-shot of her. And the third time, we go to a close-up: but not of her face; of her roller-skate.

Many people have commented on the extraordinary power of the image of this little girl. Yet what is the reason for it? For me, some of the mystery resides in this close-up. One might argue that the cut to the roller-skate is simply a crude signal to the audience, who might perhaps need it to identify her as the girl who recovered the ball from the shelter. But even if this were so, what the film presents us with is the skate as the object of *Dennis*'s regard. What does he see there? An image of impaired mobility, perhaps – a metaphor for Johnny? After all, the fact that she does not join in the scrimmage with the boys is not in itself a reason for him to attribute secret knowledge to her – except that she herself is, as James de Felice has remarked, 'an odd one out'.[8] But when we tilt up from the roller-skate, she backs into the shadow in a move echoing that of Johnny when the young lovers came into the shelter; and not only that, but for a few brief yet startling frames – an effect which cannot have been planned but is surely there – her face assumes a strong resemblance to Mason's. Again, when Dennis does come to question her, she answers wordlessly, with only nods and shakes of the head, as if in sympathy with Johnny's reduced verbal powers. But for all that, she does communicate the information; and for all the seeming club-footedness of the one skate, she slides effortlessly out of the picture – in both senses – when Dennis asks her to lead him to Johnny's lair. As I ran through this scene, I was suddenly reminded of the simplicity of St Mark's account of the arrival of the three Marys at the sepulchre: 'they saw a young man sitting on the right side, clothed in a long white garment; and they were affrighted'. (It is only 'they were affrighted' that tells us there was anything out of the ordinary about the young man; but it leaves us wondering whether, though the Marys did not consider the possibility, he may himself have been the risen Christ.)[9] It would be fanciful to claim the little girl as the angel at Johnny's not yet vacated tomb; but in view of the intrusion of Christian mythology in the later passages of this film, it might not be excessively so.

Entering the shelter, Dennis strikes a match and sees Johnny hunched on the bench. As he stoops to examine his wound, Johnny asks about the fate of the cashier:

'Did I kill that man?'

'Can you walk?'

'Did I?'

'Here, stand up – grip my arm ...'

A car brakes nearby. Dennis goes to the entrance and sees police swarming. He quickly gives Johnny instructions to wait until he hears three shots in quick fire, then make for the house – the coast will be clear. He careers off as Johnny is asking, 'Dennis – did I kill that fellow?'

When Dennis has climbed the scaffolding to the roof of a building, having now drawn all the police to the road in front of it, he pauses at the staircase door to fire the three shots; and after the first we cut to Johnny in the entrance to the shelter, blood glistening on his coat. It is a cut which any editor will appreciate (though in fact, unusually for such a small detail, it was specified in the pre-production script).[10] Not only does it emphasise the pain of Johnny's injury; there is also a subliminal suggestion that it does not ultimately matter whose bullet caused his suffering; that there is little to choose between enemy and friend. Mechanically he walks forward out of the shelter, his hair blown back by a wind which seems to exist for him alone. At this point we hear in the music a theme which will become closely associated with Johnny and with his wanderings. The theme has in fact received a full exposition over the opening titles, and has been hinted at since; but this is the first time it has, as it were, locked on to Johnny; and a profound sense of fatality lurks in its having been already present, waiting for him. (This is not the only instance of a structural use of fatality. When, in the scene before the raid, Johnny remarks that it will snow later, this is not information we need; and a first-time viewer may well have forgotten it by the time the snow does come. But it adds to our reception of the snow as fulfilment of a destiny. There is, needless to say, nothing intrinsically fatalistic about Johnny's awareness of the weather report. It is the ordering of things in the narration that counts.)

Dennis, in an empty street, stoops to stuff his bandage down a drain. But he is seen by two policemen as they emerge from a side alley. As Dennis hurries away to board a crowded tram, the policemen fish out the bandage. There follows a bravura fight scene on the tram, a jolly woman's 'Come in and warm yourself, Constable' resonating with Theresa's earlier greeting to Pat and Nolan in a mocking comment on the very idea of home and comfort. Dennis is eventually captured and dragged away into the distance: this shot being held for long enough for us to understand it as the end of a chapter.

. . . .

A gut-turning key change in the music, and we are back with Johnny trudging forward through the rain. A lorry looms up behind him and hoots. With a couple of cross-cuts of his disoriented figure from the lorry-driver's viewpoint, the lorry passes and he falls to the ground. Two women – soon to be identified as Rosie and Maudie (Fay Compton and Beryl Measor) – have witnessed this, and assume that Johnny has been struck and injured by the lorry. They help him to his feet and take him into their nearby house: 'We know all about first aid. We were in the ARP.'

The scene indoors, which follows, is distinctly strange. It begins with a shot from behind Johnny as the two prepare to examine his wound, and there is some cross-talk between them about their respective competence at first aid, and whether or not his arm is broken. But this shot is held for rather longer than one would expect; and when we do cut to Johnny, it is so briefly as to do little but emphasise the avoidance of him; and when we cut back to Rosie, it is to see that she is not returning his look. We cut again to Johnny, who says, 'Can I stay here? It's quiet.' And again Rosie does not react to him, but gets Maudie to help her stand him up and take off his coat. As Rosie begins to cut away the sleeve of Johnny's jacket, Maudie says: 'Cutting a good jacket like that? You shouldn't do that without asking him ...' Yet this is said without so much as a glance up in his direction. Not only is the camera pointedly avoiding Johnny, but the two women are talking about him – in the way some adults will talk about children in their presence – as if he were not there.

When Rosie finally gets a proper look at Johnny's injury, she stands up and backs slowly away; then she moves forward and round behind Johnny to open his jacket for Maudie to see. Of course, there is a practical reason for this awkward movement (throughout which Johnny himself is scarcely visible): it is to avoid showing us what must be assumed to be a wound so terrible that, even had the film-makers wished to reveal it, it would not have been acceptable within the censorship restrictions of the time. But all the same, this is of a piece

The wounded Johnny in the house of Rosie and Maudie

with the handling of the sequence in general. Johnny says, 'You see to it. Don't call a doctor', and Rosie says, 'I shouldn't like to interfere with that'; but this is said to Maudie, not as a reply to him. Johnny tries to stand, and we cut to the two women, who are half turned away from us. Maudie, glancing in his direction, says, 'Look at him!' and turns away as soon as she has said it, while Rosie looks almost reluctantly over her shoulder as if perhaps at an animal they knew they were going to have to put out of its misery.

As we cut to Johnny saying 'Help me up', we get the first real eye-contact in the sequence, and it brings a real, if temporary, sense of relief. There is an exchange about whether he has any friends they can go to for help. Then Rosie reaches into the pocket of Johnny's overcoat, ostensibly in search of some address or identification, and she slowly draws out the gun. Most films would bring in the music at this point; and its absence here is almost a dramatic effect in itself. 'Why should I be the one to bring you in? What will my husband say when he sees you?' Rosie puts down the gun with enormous care and moves back to confer with Maudie, revealing that she has realised who Johnny is. Off-screen, he asks, 'Did that fellow die? Did I kill him?' and Rosie nods

Rosie draws the gun from Johnny's pocket

slightly; but again, the reply is directed to Maudie, and Johnny is not meant to see.

The two withdraw into the kitchen to discuss what is to be done – Johnny now only a figure in the far background. Then Rosie's husband Tom (Arthur Hambling) arrives home. It is only when *he* sees the gun that the music begins: a brief statement of the 'fate' theme, which is immediately cut off as Tom withdraws into the kitchen and shuts the door. He and Rosie begin arguing about what is to be done with Johnny, and we can still hear their voices as he struggles to his feet, the camera tilting up to hold him in an extreme low-angle shot partly anticipated in the opening sequence when, standing up on the bed, he said to Dennis, 'Do I look soft, then?' It is at this moment that he hears, in the midst of the harangue from next door, Tom saying, 'I'm thinking about the decent man he killed', and Rosie replying, 'But he's dying now, Tom.' And the music begins in earnest.

Trying to drag his coat from the back of a chair, Johnny pulls the chair over; and the crash alerts the others, who emerge from the kitchen. From Tom's viewpoint we see Johnny, back to camera, struggling clumsily with one hand to draw back the curtain of the front door. Rosie comes along the passageway and turns to face him in the first 'normal' two-shot of the sequence – two people actually looking at each other – as he says that he is going, and that they won't have to worry about him any more. Maudie drapes his coat over his shoulders, and Tom hurries to bring a whisky bottle from which he takes a few gulps; then the door is opened, and he goes out into the howling wind. The rain is now torrential. Maudie, on Tom's instructions, comes out to drop the pistol down a stormwater drain, then runs forward to put a flat cap on Johnny's head. She runs back into the house as he departs.

For reasons which will become clear later, I have placed stress upon one aspect of the foregoing sequence: the way in which Johnny, though the focus of its activity, is almost severed from significance in it by the nature of the set-ups and the way they are put together. But there is something else about it which deserves to be mentioned, and that is its extreme theatricality. This is largely a matter of performance. When Rosie draws the gun from Johnny's pocket, she does so as if signalling the action to the back row of the circle; and both Fay Compton and Beryl Measor were, of course, known primarily for their careers on the stage. The employment of stage actors in films, particularly in 'character' roles, was not at all uncommon; but Reed seems to have been particularly keen on spreading his net as widely as possible, and to have delighted in recruiting children, animals, all-in wrestlers and various other non-professionals, as well as actors from quite a variety of backgrounds. Thus in *Odd Man Out* we have Robert Beatty, a Canadian well established in British cinema, and Kathleen Ryan, who had never been in a film before, mingling with stalwarts of Dublin's Abbey Theatre as well as some genuine natives of Belfast. As for James Mason, it is entirely possible that when we watch his performance today, refracted as it is through our knowledge of the serious roles he undertook in his later years, we are seeing something slightly different from what viewers would have seen at the time, knowing only his background as a saturnine man-you-love-to-hate figure in Gainsborough costume dramas. As one critic put it before the film was even released: 'The sadistic young man who used a riding crop on Margaret Lockwood in *Man in Grey*, socked Dulcie Gray in *They Were Sisters* and damaged Ann Todd's fingers in *Seventh Veil* is now having a tough time himself.'[11]

But it is not only that Reed chooses actors from varying and even contrasting traditions; having done so, he is happy to let them perform in their own styles and does not attempt to impose conformity on them. Thus Cusack is allowed his moment of comic inebriation, just as Compton is allowed to back away in horror from Johnny's injury as if she were starring in *Murder in the Red Barn*. But it is impossible to imagine the two in the same scene. I think this approach to actors is part of a broader characteristic of Reed's work which I would describe as a taste for the heterogeneous. When you have a character switch on a radio at random, anything may come out of it; but to give us Schubert's 'Unfinished' in Theresa's house was surely a master-stroke of incongruity. It is like the jokes, or like the somewhat cavalier integration of studio with location shots, or like the deadpan little boy who punctuates Dennis's questioning of the otherwise raucous children with a repeated 'Give us a penny, mister.' Few would deny that Reed's work, in spite of the perhaps damaging heterogeneity of his total oeuvre, has a distinctive flavour; and this is as near as I can come to identifying what it is: a quality of the full-blooded and all-welcoming. He seems to have recognised that there is no *right* way for the film to represent human experience, and to have been content to allow the conventions to jostle, to give what they had to offer, and to live as good neighbours or bad.

2

....

We have reached a nodal point in the film, where much that has happened will alter the character of what is to come. Johnny now knows that he is a murderer, and has overheard a reference to himself as 'dying'. The comrades who might have attempted to rescue him are either arrested or dead; and henceforth his encounters will be more random and outlandish, the motives of those who seek him more secretive and questionable. The police, of course, are still after him; but even they will come to be more personalised in the inscrutable figure of the Inspector. Johnny is setting out in a coat worn cloakwise and a new hat; but his arm is bandaged as was Dennis's when he sought to mislead the police by impersonating him. Night and foul weather have driven the children indoors. It would almost be possible to feel that Johnny's death had occurred at the moment of his expulsion from Rosie's house, and that the remainder of the film was taking place in purgatory.

Johnny staggers forward alongside a parked horse-cab, and tries to open the door. With a clatter of boots, three soldiers run towards us from under an arch, joking together in London accents; and one of them stops to ask Johnny if he is all right and to help him into the shelter of the cab. The other soldiers have paused some way further on, and there is some shouted badinage about whether Johnny is ill or tight. The first soldier smells his breath and exclaims 'Ah, lovely!' – perhaps in ironic reference to the once ubiquitous 'Ah, Bisto!' poster. Then they see their tram passing the end of the street, and clatter off again. This minuscule scene manages exquisitely to encapsulate the camaraderie of barrack life. Yet no sooner have the men turned to run off than we cut to the cabbie emerging from a café. Such brusque handling of transitions, in which no time is allowed for an action to play itself out, is characteristic of Reed's narrative style – and, to an extent, of that of the period. But it takes on a particular resonance within the episodic structure of *Odd Man Out*. We remember the little girl who in less than a second skated out of our universe. Our interest in people is ruthlessly truncated once they have done what the story requires of them.

Seen through the misty window of his vehicle, the cabbie picks up a rain-sodden carnation and pokes it into his button-hole. His gesture would be at home in a sentimental operetta, where he might retrieve a bloom the young lovers had carelessly discarded. Thus accoutred, he drives Johnny innocently, and on the strength of a little banter, through the police cordon. Briefly, as it moves away, we are struck by the cab's resemblance to a hearse.

....

Back at the house, Kathleen and Granny are waiting. Granny, looking through the window, sees a police car pull up outside; and Kathleen, remembering that there is a gun upstairs, goes to 'get rid of it' even while Granny moves to answer the knock on the door. The next few shots will be characterised by such urgency – by things happening in the nick of time. The police come in saying they have orders to search the house. Kathleen retrieves the gun from a drawer and, in a gesture which tells us she is familiar with firearms, flicks open the cylinder to check if it is loaded. As a policeman is approaching up the stairs, Kathleen slips behind the bedroom door and puts on a jacket which is hanging there. The policeman, finding her behind the door, tells her to wait downstairs, where two other policemen are moving from room to room. While both have their backs turned, Granny takes the gun and hides it up her sleeve; and Kathleen, noticing the bandage on the table, takes it away and puts it on the mantelpiece. As she does so, we hear the click of the latch. Cold as moonlight, the Inspector enters, glances around as if instantly taking in everything he needed to know, and asks simply: 'Where is he?'

The Inspector questions Kathleen about Johnny, implying that failure to tell what she knows could make her an accessory to murder: 'I know they've been here, smoking cigarettes and drinking tea, the whole bunch of them. ... You were making plans how you could find him – that's the truth now, isn't it?' Theresa of course has talked; but it will be a part of the Inspector's strangeness always to seem to know a little bit more than is accounted for by the information at his disposal. Just before he orders the men to search the room they are in, there occurs a curious snatch of dialogue:

KATHLEEN: What do you want me to say?

INSPECTOR: I want the truth, that's all.
KATHLEEN: You want to know where he is?
INSPECTOR: Yes.
KATHLEEN: I'm ready.

Ready for what? Not to reveal the information – which in any case she does not possess. Ready to be taken in for questioning? Perhaps. When the others have finished, and have been told to leave, there is an even more intense passage of questioning, in which the Inspector makes it clear, albeit indirectly, that he knows Kathleen is in love with Johnny. This is handled, with hushed speech and seemingly wilful lack of emotion, in two-shot followed by cross-cut close-ups, almost as if it were a scene between two young people afraid to confess their true feelings to one another. And the hypnotic spell is broken only when the Inspector turns abruptly saying, 'Stay out of this business!' and leaves, slamming the door behind him. Are we being told that the Inspector is attracted to Kathleen? There is little to substantiate this, and there are other possible explanations for his behaviour – especially when we learn, later, that he hails from the same community as the rebels. On the whole, it seems to me more in keeping with the way this film works to see the scene as asserting an iconographic kinship between the two characters: a chill at the bone, a shared pitilessness in the pursuit of objectives – and even in the objectives themselves.

Immediately upon the Inspector's departure, Kathleen takes off the jacket and puts on her outdoor coat. She says to Granny, 'Give me the revolver'; and, when Granny tries to remonstrate with her, insists with, 'Let me have what I want.' Sensitised as we already are to Kathleen's manner, we may find in this form of words something more frightening, because more universal, than a simple demand for a gun. Taking Kathleen's hands in hers, Granny begins a long speech about the hopelessness of going off and looking for men like Johnny. We cut, on her cue, to an oval-framed photograph of herself in a wedding dress: 'I had the fine looks, the same as you have them now ...' Music begins hauntingly as we pan up from the photograph to see Kathleen reflected in the mirror over the mantelpiece. 'I had the boys admiring me. There was Hughie Fitzpatrick – he wanted to marry me, so he did ...' At this point Kathleen notices her own reflection, and we track slowly in on her as she holds her own gaze. 'He was a rebel on the run and was never

seen again. Did I go out to look for him? I did not.' Kathleen looks down again. 'I stayed and had my life ...' – we cut back to Granny – 'and grand times I had.'

Kathleen regards Granny with impassivity. From the words, as one may imagine them on the page of the script, it might be assumed that Kathleen was motivated by disapproval of her grandmother's willingness to let the menfolk go for the sake of a happy life; but the way the scene is put together tells a different story. The underlining with music of the moment when Kathleen, looking into her own eyes, identifies her youth with the lost youth of her grandmother; the coincidence of this with the words 'He was a rebel on the run, and was never seen again'; the fact that Granny's wedding picture has no husband in it, as if she had somehow been the bride of the missing man; even the loss of her acclaimed beauty behind the conventional photographic retouching of her era: all these combine powerfully to suggest, in a manner oblique to the primary sense of the dialogue, that what Kathleen wants is to disappear into martyrdom and into myth.

. . . .

Granny having talked herself to sleep, Kathleen takes the gun from her sleeve, strokes her hair in a brief moment of tenderness, then leaves the house. There is a mix to the horse-cab moving along the crowded street: 'Cab, sir. Cab, sir.' A man and woman hail it, then complain that there is already someone inside. The cabbie dismounts and discovers Johnny. In one of the several moments of irony which enable this film to keep melodrama at arm's-length, the cabbie is just protesting to Johnny that he cannot possibly risk carrying him any further when a traffic policeman shouts at him to 'get along, there'. He climbs back into the driving seat and moves off.

Eventually, having seen Kathleen combing the empty streets in the vicinity of the shelters, we arrive with the cab at a desolate builder's yard, the music fading out as the clock, seen some way off, chimes the three-quarter. In the pouring rain, the cabbie eases Johnny out of the vehicle, murmuring – absurdly – 'Come on, son, you'll be all right here.' Johnny, who appears to be asleep, falls onto the cobbles; and the cabbie has to half-carry him into the yard, where he dumps him into an iron hip bath under the benediction of a tilted stone angel and the mournful clangour of distant trains.

It is an ending of sorts – or could be. The world seems deserted.
But as the cabbie climbs up towards us onto his seat, he registers
surprise; and we cut to a shot looking down upon a dishevelled, skinny
man wearing a threadbare scarf and a battered bowler: 'I saw you, Gin.
Is he hurt bad?' The cabbie retorts, 'You keep out of this, Shell', and
gees up his horse. And then, in yet another of this film's unpredictable
changes of manner, a sprightly yet mocking little tune is introduced by
the bassoon as Shell (F. J. McCormick) glances around, takes a few
hopping steps in Johnny's direction, hesitates, moves away along the
street, then swings around a lamp-post to return and go into the yard.
He stops alongside the angel, sees Johnny, appears to recognise him –
and scampers off again.

Kathleen is hurrying along a dockside crowded with embarking
and disembarking passengers. She passes through a gate into a less
populous area, where goods are being loaded; and she tries to persuade
a seaman – perhaps the master of a fishing vessel – to wait for her to
bring Johnny and, by implication, to help them escape. Uneasily, the
seaman promises to ensure that the gate at the foot of the clock tower
will be left open; but he says he will be sailing soon after eleven. I have
seen *Odd Man Out* quite a few times, yet I always manage to forget this
plot point about the waiting ship. One contributory reason may be that,
although there must be a rendezvous arranged if only so that it can be
missed, we already know by this stage in the film that the conclusion
towards which it is building would be negated if Johnny were to
survive.

....

Seen in close-up through the windscreen of his advancing car, the
Inspector wipes the mist from the glass as he peers towards the
pavement where, in the following shot, we see Kathleen among
hurrying pedestrians. The car pulls up just ahead of her, and the
Inspector gets out: 'Out for a little walk, I suppose.' Kathleen ignores
him and walks out of the picture. In one smooth movement, the
Inspector gets back into the car as a plainclothes policeman gets out
from the rear door to follow her.

Kathleen crosses a main road towards a brightly lit dance-hall.
She seems about to continue past it, but then – knowing or guessing
that she is being followed – takes a sudden turn and runs up the steps

and through the swing doors. To the blare of a band endlessly repeating an inane riff, she weaves through the hectic dancers and leaves again by the fire exit. This little scene – a single shot which begins on the notice 'No Jitterbugging', tilts down to pick up Kathleen entering the mêlée in the left foreground and pans around with her to the other door – carries distant echoes of a Hitchcock thriller, or even of the entry into a noisy saloon in a Western (where the notice would probably say 'All Hardware Must be Left at the Counter'). If I have several times drawn attention to such echoes, which are seldom emphatic enough to be treated as quotations or intertextual references, it is not only to suggest the breadth of the film's stylistic catchment. While the genres evoked may not always have anything specific to offer, by way of irony or otherwise, each new stylistic signal demands of us a microscopic readjustment of our response, of our awareness of the ways life may be shown; and this cognitive restlessness helps to keep us receptive to the meanings which criss-cross the narrative like treacherous rogue currents. It also, I think, readies us for the film's major shifts of register, such as that which occurs as Johnny leaves the sanctuary of Rosie's house.

Kathleen runs down the steps of the dance-hall, but resignedly slows her pace as she hears the door slam again behind her. The plainclothes man catches up with her as they are passing a graveyard beyond which, once again, the clock-tower is seen. The fact that the clock-tower is visible from so many of the locations – and its chimes audible equally from practically all of them – serves to define the action as occurring within a very restricted space: a space at variance, or so it seems to me, with the insistence upon police cars, with the distances apparently travelled and with the panorama of the opening aerial images. There is something of the fairy tale about this spatial compression, magically superimposed upon the normal geography of the city, in which, however far you go, you will never find yourself very much further from the clock.

Having failed to persuade Kathleen of the uselessness of visiting Father Tom – whom we have heard her mention to the seaman as someone who may know what has become of Johnny – the plainclothes man rings the bell for her at the door of his residence and leaves her there, and the housekeeper lets her in. As Father Tom (W. G. Fay) comes into the hallway to meet her, he says, 'You came to ask me about

Johnny McQueen'; and through the open door in the background we see Shell lean forward into view. Kathleen asks Father Tom if he knows Johnny, and he answers, 'I taught him as a child ... I know them all.' Then he adds: 'I've another visitor – a poor man whose bird is sick. We'd better hear what he's got to say first.' The atmosphere here is very strange, almost as if Kathleen were being received into heaven, but a heaven dowdier than she had imagined it. Partly this is to do with Father Tom's placid manner, his apparent willingness to defer the urgent question of Johnny in favour of that of a sick bird; but it is also the fact that he 'knows' why she has come. Since it is made clear that (somewhat surprisingly) he is not already acquainted with Kathleen, this cannot be an entirely rational conclusion on his part. As with some of the Inspector's deductions, it carries just a hint of the supernatural.

It is worth bearing in mind that the idea of the supernatural was something of a commonplace in films of that period. (We may recall the upsurge of interest in spiritualism which occurred in the later years of the war, when many people who had lost loved ones in circumstances which ruled out the normal *rites de passage* of hospital, tears by the bedside and the disposal of mortal remains were perhaps unable to feel

Father Tom (W. G. Fay)

that the dead had truly departed.) It appears at its most literal and dire in *The Halfway House* (Dearden, 1944), is employed as an available convention in *A Matter of Life and Death* (Powell/Pressburger, 1946), attains something of an apotheosis in *Dead of Night* (Cavalcanti and others, 1945) and crops up even in such an unlikely context as *Fires Were Started* (Jennings, 1943). I would not want to make too much of this; but I do suggest that a soupçon of the supernatural is one of the lesser elements which contribute to the mix of *Odd Man Out*, and that its function is, as with some others we have noted, to help keep it – like films we saw in childhood and did not quite understand – always just a fraction beyond our reckoning.

Shell has a caged budgerigar on his knee, and is expatiating upon its rare qualities. Kathleen, standing against the window with the clock-tower prominent beyond, betrays impatience. But soon she begins to recognise that his words have a double meaning, and that he is using the bird as a metaphor for Johnny. She and Father Tom play along with this in order to learn as much as possible from him. It becomes clear that he knows where Johnny is, but that, though he prefers not to claim the reward from the police, he expects some financial benefit from the transaction: 'Of course, I know there's prayer and all that; but if I don't take what's coming to me as chances, I'm finished. I'll just starve, and that's a fact.' Father Tom insists that there is no money available, but offers instead to try to inspire in him 'a precious particle of faith'. Shell seems puzzled by this, and ask whether faith will 'pay the rent for me and help me to get a pint of stout now and then'. Is this meant sarcastically? It seems not. Yet it is hard to credit that someone brought up in that milieu, even if not himself a churchgoer, would never have encountered the concept of faith. For all his quirkiness, Shell has not been portrayed as a simpleton.

This is, for me, the only moment when the film really falters. In fact it is approaching one of its stylistic cusps; but we have received no signal of that, and are still responding in terms of a psychological realism about to be superseded. Thus when Shell decides to accept Father Tom's bargain, we are left asking the wrong questions: questions unhelpful to our understanding, such as whether he has done so just because he realises he has failed to strike a better bargain, or whether he genuinely does not know that 'faith' has no cash value – in which case, it might be argued, Father Tom has seriously deceived him.

Shell sets out to fetch Johnny; and Kathleen says, in the same tone as when demanding the gun from Granny, 'Father, when Shell returns, give Johnny to me.' Father Tom replies that all he wants is to hear Johnny's confession and 'to do what I can to comfort his soul', and that afterwards he will try to persuade him to give himself up. When Kathleen tries to protest, he says: 'What do you want me to do, child – help you to take him back to the boys, so that he'll kill more people and defy the authorities?' We realise at this moment that the serenity with which Father Tom has seemed endowed is little more than indifference to the human rigmarole. The lighting in this shot stresses his age and feebleness; and we see him as a husk of a man, wedded to his duties, whose imagination cannot stretch to the possibility – for us, as viewers, virtually a condition of the coherence of the narrative – that Johnny, if he were to be saved, would not 'kill more people'.

Kathleen comments that she would kill Johnny, and herself with him, rather than let him fall into the hands of the police. This statement, naturally, scandalises the priest; and there follows a disputation about the ethics of killing. In the entire exchange, in the entire scene, Kathleen's only statement not overtly anticipating death is when she says, 'I can take him away from all of them and be with him. You will never hear of him again.' But this is a phrasing which recalls Granny's reminiscences about the suitor who 'was never seen again': the moment eerily marked by the look in the mirror. Some critics have found this passage overlong. But it has the merit of leaving us in no doubt about Kathleen's preoccupations. Is it any wonder that we forget she has a plan for Johnny's rescue?

. . . .

It is snowing. A distant train wails past; and as Johnny wakes, his music begins. He tries to rise out of the hip bath, and falls on his face in the mud. Struggling to his feet, be begins walking. He crosses the road towards the bright beacon of a telephone kiosk in which are two flashy young women, one of them engaged in animated but inaudible conversation. Johnny pauses as if hoping to make a call; but there are two policemen approaching, and he moves on. The two women have meanwhile noticed him: just one flicker of human curiosity before they return to their own concerns. As with the young couple in the air-raid shelter, the poignancy of the world Johnny can no longer share is manifested for us through its plainness. The *total* inaudibility of the women's speech – which in reality would have been muted – is a product of the progressive elimination of natural sounds when the music is present: which is to say that, to a degree, Johnny's state of mind is coming to be mirrored in the fabric of the film.

We track back with Johnny as he passes people hunched against the snow, bumping into them in the flurries, his bandage unwinding out of his sleeve. The music gives way to hubbub as he enters a huge Victorian pub and crosses immediately into one of the cubicles. The publican, Fencie, is played by William Hartnell, an actor who specialised in tense characters – typically sergeants – desperate to keep their world in check with the twitch of a cheek muscle. He has seen Johnny come in, tries to force some spirits down him and barks at him to leave; then, realising he is stuck with him till closing time, shuts him in the cubicle and wedges the latch with a discarded cigarette packet.

The half-hour chimes as Shell scurries across a street and into a building. He climbs an ample, ambassadorial staircase, dodging past a doorway through which Lukey (Robert Newton) is seen painting, and up to the top landing where a sift of snow falls steadily from a smashed

Production still of William Hartnell as Fencie

4 6   Shell (F. J. McCormick) with the budgerigar

rococo skylight. Indeed, the place seems open to the elements at the front too. In a film where sound is used with great care, if not always with strict realism, we must surely count it significant that we hear no front door opening or closing when people arrive or leave. It is the architecture, as much as anything, which tells us we have entered a new phase of the story: one, perhaps, in which Shell will take his place among O'Casey's garrulous deadbeats for whom the function of language is to generate a fog in which meanings may be faintly discerned floundering.

Shell enters a room full of cages of budgerigars, which start twittering as soon as the light is switched on and stop as soon as it is switched off, deposits his birdcage among the others and tries to creep back downstairs again. But he is waylaid on the lower landing by Lukey, who wants him to pose for an unfinished painting of St Francis preaching to the birds. In an attempt to extricate himself, Shell confides that he knows where Johnny McQueen is hidden, and that he has 'agreed on terms' for delivering him to Father Tom. Lukey grabs him: 'I'm going to hit you hard for selling a man that's on the run. ... I'm going to hit you hard, unless – unless you bring him to me to paint.'

Lukey (Robert Newton) wreathed in smoke

The moment Lukey has let go of him, Shell darts for the door. As he runs down the staircase, he passes Tober (Elwyn Brook Jones), who is ascending with stately lack of haste.

Lukey is seated at the stove in the studio as Tober enters behind him. Tober asks if there are faces in the fire, and he replies, 'Hundreds of them, Tober: beautiful ones, ugly ones, smiling, glaring at me, men and women one after another telling me things, shedding tears; but they don't stay.' And as he says this, his own face is wreathed in the smoke.

. . . .

Shell, in consternation, searches the yard for Johnny, then moves away into the street where, attempting to cross the road, he is narrowly missed by a car, a bicycle, another car. We track back along the street with him, as previously we did with Johnny, until his attention is caught by something off-screen; and, as we cut to a shot of the bandage coiled around a lamp-post, a few brief notes of the 'fate' theme are sufficient to confirm its association with Johnny. Shell picks up the bandage. In a bizarre gesture, almost as if he were a tracker-dog, he sniffs it. Then he becomes aware of the pub entrance, and goes in.

A characteristic movement of Shell is to keep turning around, in tight little cycles, as he progresses; and now, approaching the bar counter at which Fencie is seen serving in the background, he notices in his gyration the jammed latch of Johnny's cubicle. As he saunters towards it, trying to see over the partition, Fencie calls, 'Shell – have a drink, Shell!' Shell moves back to the counter, but we are left to assume that Fencie's unaccustomed generosity has given the game away.

Shell does his budgerigar routine with Fencie, and is just about to reach some arrangement with him when Lukey enters the pub. Shell tries not to be seen by him as Lukey orders a drink and starts talking about Johnny. And now we cut to Johnny in the cubicle, his head resting on the table. Turning, he knocks over a glass. The beer dregs spread in bubbles on the table-top; and in the bubbles, as he stares at them, appear the faces of the cashier, the cabbie, the soldier, all addressing him directly, repeating their simple lines; and these are joined by Kathleen, and by Rosie's husband, until there is nothing but a cacophony of voices all speaking at once. Johnny leans back, sweeping the glass from the table; and over a wide shot of the customers in the pub, he gives vent to a great howl of desperation which leaves utter

Above: A wide shot of customers in the pub
Overleaf: Johnny's great howl of desperation

silence behind it. But in this silence, just as we are wondering what can possibly happen next, Lukey catches sight of Shell – 'There's that little rat!' – and we are pitched into a classic bar-room brawl complete with comic shots of the barmen swivelling like shooting gallery mannequins as Shell, unseen, scoots past them under the counter.

Shell eventually makes his escape. The pub is cleared, and Lukey is told that in payment for the damage he has caused he will have to take responsibility for the removal of Johnny. A horse-cab is ordered, and they all help bundle him into it – one barman muttering, 'It's ten years if we're caught.'

. . . .

Back in the studio, Tober is stretched in a chair before the stove eating fish and chips. Shell enters, holding his lip for Tober to see, and asking if the damage is serious: 'When you were a student in that university in Dublin, you learned about things like this.' It will gradually emerge that Tober, though once a medical student, never completed his studies. 'Am I hurt bad?' Being 'hurt bad' is the phrase he constantly uses in reference to Johnny. Tober's manner is very English, very public school. Though he'll toss a spare packet of fish and chips to Shell, his reaction to being told of the spoiled plan to take Johnny to Father Tom is, 'To get your dirty bit of profit?' And to the rejoinder – 'Well, I have to live' – 'Shell, you are foul.'

When Shell asks Tober what 'faith' means, he replies, 'Only one man had it.' Does he mean Jesus? I am no theologian; but as I understand it, Christianity enjoins its followers to have faith in the redemptive power of Jesus's sacrifice; and to refer to Jesus as the only person who possessed faith strikes a rather odd note. When pressed on the meaning of the word, Tober adds – even less helpfully – 'It's life.' In such a context as this, questions about the likelihood of Shell's being already familiar with the concept do not even occur to us: a confirmation of just how stylistically watertight these episodes are. And what are we to make of the following exchange between Tober and Lukey, when the latter has brought Johnny back and has begun to paint him?

LUKEY: I understand what I see in him.
TOBER: What is it?

LUKEY: The truth about us all.
TOBER: Is that all?
LUKEY: He's doomed.
TOBER: So are we all.
SHELL: Is he really dying, Tober?
TOBER: We're all dying.

Words have come adrift from their moorings; and it should hardly surprise us that, nearly a quarter of a century later, Harold Pinter made explicit reference to this film, and to the roles of Newton and McCormick, in his play *Old Times*.[12]

By now, Johnny is seated on a chair on a dais, and Lukey, who has turned a harsh light on him, has begun painting. Tober, meanwhile, has begun in a businesslike way to clean and dress his wounds, attended by Shell, who brings hot water and 'all them silver scissors'. While Lukey jams a palette behind Johnny's head to stop it falling back, Shell asks, 'Have you got the stuff that makes the smell in hospitals?'

....

Johnny seated for his portrait

Father Tom is drinking soup. The city clock, seen through the window, shows 10.45. Kathleen glances down at the sound of a car arriving, and closes the curtain quickly as the Inspector alights. Father Tom tells her he will receive him downstairs, and goes to intercept the Inspector in the hallway and take him into the vestry. His greeting, 'Hello, Fred', is all that is needed for us to understand that he has known him, as he has known the rebels, from childhood: and once more our attention is directed to childhood as spawning-ground for the differentiations of later life. Indeed, the period between childhood and death in this film seems scarcely more than the eight hours of the story's span.

While Father Tom potters around him, taking a chair from a pile, shutting the connecting door to the church, the Inspector stands with his cap under one arm, the other hand resting on his cane, in the frozen attitude of a public statue. Questions about Johnny's movements and about the culpability of Kathleen lead nowhere. Eventually Father Tom says, 'You might think this strange, but I wish I could have seen him before his arrest. I wanted so much to comfort him.' The Inspector replies, as we track in towards him: 'That isn't unreasonable, Father, but you can't do that unless he's coming here.' (Again, it is a conclusion not entirely warranted by the information at his command.) For the first and only time in the film, the Inspector smiles, and his smile is a devilish one.

As this is happening, Kathleen slips away. She runs to the now deserted dock gates. Back in the vestry, the Inspector tells Father Tom that he is going to have the streets in the vicinity watched, and advises him to keep 'that young woman' with him for a while. He leaves, and we return to the docks where Kathleen is persuading the seaman to extend his deadline till midnight: 'I'll get him before then.' It is now eleven o'clock.

. . . .

Back in the studio, with the clock's chimes continuing from the previous scene, we find Johnny seated in majesty on the dais as Tober completes the bandaging of his arm. (The bandaging of arms has become something of a leitmotif. This third time, the bandage will survive its wearer.) Lukey is painting, but his own bulk obscures the canvas from us. Shell, seated reverentially before Tober, speculates on the affluent life he could have led if only he had finished his studies:

'You'd have had the top hat, and fine clothes, and a big house ...'
Behind Shell, when the camera settles on him, is one of Lukey's
portraits of him, likewise in battered bowler and muffler: as if it were
the start of a set of mirrorings in which his hopelessness might be
replicated for ever.

Johnny tries to stand up; but Tober, rising more quickly as his
work is done, pushes him firmly back and announces, 'He's ready for
hospital now, Lukey.' Lukey protests that Johnny is not fit to be moved,
and Tober becomes angry at his wanting to keep a man for painting
who needs a blood transfusion. Lukey retorts that Tober only wants to
get Johnny to hospital so as to show off his skills, and Shell dives in to
accuse the pot of calling the kettle black. We cut to Johnny, and move in
on him. The off-screen voices become jumbled, and music starts. The
camera begins making tight circling movements, and we cut to Johnny's
view of the studio lined with paintings, its perspective expression-
istically distorted. Then, as the voices begin talking about the police,
and about Johnny's prospects of being put up for trial, the paintings
detach themselves from the walls and arrange themselves as a jury, or
as a congregation, before us.

Lukey painting Johnny

We cut back to Johnny, and Shell whispers to him, 'Have you ever heard tell of Father Tom?' The mention of Father Tom seems to ease Johnny's delirium – though the off-screen voices are now going in circles, the same phrases mechanically recurring. The image of Father Tom appears among the paintings, and Johnny leans forward: 'Tell me, Father, like you used to tell us . . .' The phantom gesticulates. 'Louder, Father, speak louder – I can't hear you.' The voices of Lukey and Tober rise to a climax, then break off abruptly on a cut to them watching. Johnny begins talking to Father Tom as if in homely reminiscence: 'Ah, we've always drowned your voice with our shouting.' (But it is the voices of Lukey and Tober that have been shouting.) 'I remember, when I was a boy . . .' The phrase sparks a recollection; and, with intercuts of the others immobile and gazing upward at him in a manner reminiscent of saints and donors at the foot of the Cross, he recites: 'When I was a child, I spoke as a child, I understood as a child; but when I became a man, I put away childish things.' (It is a statement so ambiguous in this context as to be almost beyond fathoming. Are the 'childish things' some vision of innocence; or are they the toy guns with which we have already seen children impersonating Johnny himself?) Then, from an already low-angle seated position, he rises to stand, the

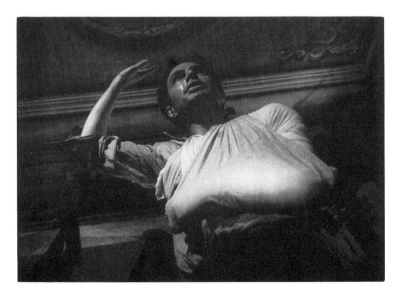

'Though I speak with the tongues of men and of angels . . .'

extreme low angle now duplicating the one when he overheard that he had killed the cashier. His hand raised above his head, a ribbon of saliva trailing from his lip, his accent sliding decidedly towards Welsh, he declaims: 'Though I speak with the tongues of men and of angels, and have not charity, I am become as sounding brass or a tinking cymbal. And though I have the gift of prophecy, and understand all mysteries, and all knowledge; and though I have faith, so that I could remove mountains, and have not charity, I am nothing.' It is a selective quotation from I Corinthians xiii.

....

James Mason describes this climactic scene as showing Johnny's recognition of the absence of charity in his life.[13] And since Carol Reed was a director noted for the closeness of his involvement with actors, we may perhaps suppose that this was his view too. If this were certain, I think we would be bound to conclude that Reed had misjudged his own work. There has been nothing to suggest that Johnny lacks charity – rather the reverse. For such an interpretation to carry weight would have required a characterisation comparable to that which Richard Attenborough brought to Pinkie in *Brighton Rock* (John Boulting, 1947).

You can see how this might have looked in a synopsis: Johnny has a vision in which Father Tom silently encourages him to remember his childhood lessons and to repent of his wickedness, nodding approval as he repeats St Paul's message . . . Without doubt I invest my own non-religious convictions into my response to the film, but I do not think I am bending the evidence if I say that the treatment of this moment quite contradicts what we might lazily suppose to be its 'intention'. Father Tom's limitations have already been made evident; and here his small spectre, mute, translucent and jerky as a marionette, can scarcely measure up to the towering figure of Johnny. Again, the biblical text states that faith is nothing without charity; but the passion of Mason's delivery leaves us with the strong impression that faith is a far *lesser* thing than charity – a meaning which St Paul surely did not intend, but which any humanist would fully endorse. Where, then, does this leave the 'precious particle of faith' promised by Father Tom? *Odd Man Out* can certainly be construed, rewardingly and with consistency, on the assumption that its Christian references are its stones rather than its architecture.

My own assumption has always been that Johnny's invocation of charity is primarily a protestation against the attributes of those who have been using him, for one purpose and another, all of them more or less selfish, throughout the story: whether to practise first aid, to chalk up one more saved soul, or to capture on canvas the light in the eyes of a dying man. There is clearly a sense in which he is himself assuming the burden of this fault – the linkage of extreme low-angle shots taking us right back to the moment when he asks, almost tenderly, 'Do I look soft, then?' – and such assumption of burden undoubtedly contributes to the parallelism which many critics have detected between his martyrdom and that of Christ. For Johnny, however, the moment of recognition is not now; it is pushed back beyond the start of the narrative to the putative time when, in prison, he lost his belief in violence.

There is something chilling in the way other characters speak of Johnny. The Inspector: 'He belongs to the law now.' Dennis: 'As long as he lives, he'll belong to the Organisation.' Kathleen: 'Sooner or later the police will get him. Let me have him until then.' Lukey: 'I want him. Afterwards you can do what you like with him.' Only Shell, whose overt motives are the most mercenary of all, invites some sympathy in his outburst against Lukey and Tober: 'You fellas are not caring a pin about him – yammering about his body and his soul.' I feel sure it was this aspect of the film – this bleak representation of a world where the mutualities which link people are severed, a world where every man *is* an island – which so upset Edgar Anstey, whose work in the Griersonian documentary movement was dedicated to the task of affirming such mutualities on the level of social structure. And he may have found it especially upsetting that such a film should have come from Carol Reed. For although Reed disavowed any political allegiance, he was arguably the only feature director of his time able to represent working-class characters without caricaturing them; and his taste for location shooting, and for the use of non-professional extras, and for the tactile qualities of genuine objects could appear inherently progressive in those days of studio-bound production when such preferences were understood almost as the hallmarks of documentary.

If there were no more to *Odd Man Out* than a denial of human interdependence, alleviated by some nebulous quality called 'artistry', we might even now be inclined to say that Anstey was right to inveigh against it. Socialist realism is not so unattractive when the socialism is real. Indeed, it may be that the film speaks more eloquently to the 1990s, when we have seen methodically dismantled the structures of social mutuality which Anstey's generation worked hard to create, than to the time in which it was produced. There can hardly be a more accurate word than 'charity' for those human impulses which capitalism scorns as dysfunctional.

3

. . . .

The narrative now approaches its resolution. Speech becomes depleted and practical as action takes over.

Tober leaves to call an ambulance. Johnny rises and attempts to steady himself by grasping a cord strung across the studio, which comes away and brings Lukey's easel crashing down with it. As Johnny walks woodenly out followed by Shell, who has promised to take him to Father Tom, Lukey is left looking miserably at his failed painting. In the background, seen through the window, is the clock.

Once more we are tracking back through the snow with Johnny,

Above: Johnny brings down the easel
Overleaf: Johnny spreadeagled – as in a crucifixion? (production still)

TC112 · 83

6 2   Production still of Kathleen and Johnny

Shell dancing and dithering ahead of him. But his strength is ebbing faster this time; and when Shell pulls him to the ground behind a garden hedge to avoid a police patrol, he loses consciousness. Shell tells him to stay where he is, and goes on alone. As he passes the clock tower – now seen, for the first time since the opening aerial shots, at its full height – we note that it reads 11.45; but we hear no chimes.

Kathleen intercepts Shell as he arrives at the church and rings the doorbell. She insists that he take her directly to Johnny; and as the housekeeper opens the door, they ask her to tell Father Tom that they have gone to the square. But meanwhile Johnny has been roused by the light falling on him as two boys open the curtain at an upstairs window; and he is again on the move.

Shell breaks a lace and loses a shoe, and Kathleen hurries on without him. Johnny passes a warehouse with the sign 'Prime Meat' and eventually reaches the dock railings, gripping them for support, spreadeagling himself against them in what some have interpreted as a crucifixion. Then at last, under an arch, with the clock in the background at 11.55, Kathleen appears around a corner and sees Johnny. She runs forward, and we cut to Johnny: 'Kathleen – is it really you?' And as she answers – 'Come to me and see' – Kathleen backs away slightly. It is a shocking moment. Granted we understand that she is encouraging him to walk, as one would encourage a toddler, the fact remains that at the very moment when film convention demands she should run to Johnny she does the opposite. Fictitious characters do not have motives, except in so far as we attribute these to them; and what we are engaged upon, as viewers, is not the interpretation of an individual's psychology but the construction of a film's meaning. It is in this overall construction that a character's actions play their part; and Kathleen's first response on finding Johnny confirms the absoluteness of his isolation in a way that will colour our view of their embrace, and of her assurance that they have a chance of escape together.

We track sideways along the railings with Kathleen and Johnny, and an almost casual glance over her shoulder cues a cut to a line of police and police-cars advancing upon us, dimly seen, their torches and headlights glimmering through the snow. The music simply continues its steady tread; and the fact that there is no extraneous emphasis placed upon this cut gives it a quality of the inevitable. I know no other film image which conveys such utter despair.

As Johnny collapses back against the railings, unable to go on, and the police continue their implacable approach, he asks, 'Is it far?' and Kathleen replies, 'It's a long way, Johnny; but I'm coming with you' – a line which in other circumstances, without the ambivalences which have been structured into the persona of Kathleen, could come across as emptily sentimental. Her final words, 'We're going away together', confirm for us that this is what she has meant all along. She draws the gun and fires twice towards the police. Shell and Father Tom, running towards the scene, halt in their tracks at the sound of the shots and an answering volley of gunfire.

The two bodies lie beside the railings. Father Tom and Shell arrive as the police crowd in from all sides. Father Tom, kneeling beside the bodies, cocks an eyebrow when the Inspector, handed the gun, notes that only two shots have been fired. This, in view of what Kathleen has said to him earlier, presumably leads him to suppose that she has been guilty of the mortal sins of murder and suicide. Surprisingly, we may owe the form of this ending to the representative of the US censor's office who, visiting Carol Reed on the set, is said to have told him it would be unacceptable for Kathleen to be shown killing

64   The line of police cars in the snow

Johnny herself. However, by this same account – which appears in Nicholas Wapshott's biography – Reed claimed to have subverted the instruction by ensuring that the shots were fired downwards; and this, to my eye at least, is contradicted by the film.[14]

The Inspector stands motionless, holding Kathleen's gun tilted towards her corpse as if in final confirmation of their symbolic twinning. Ignoring him, Father Tom gets up wearily, puts an arm round Shell's shoulder and walks away. But we do not hold on him. Instead, we tilt up to the city clock as it chimes midnight.

. . . .

We must confront the question of the presence of Christian symbols in *Odd Man Out*. Is it real or imaginary? If real, what is its significance? I have noted one or two seeming allusions to the Christian story, and I might add that the position of Johnny's raised hand when he speaks the words of St Paul is reminiscent of that of the Christ in Michelangelo's *Last Judgment*.[15] Several critics have referred to Johnny's progress as a *via dolorosa*. One might reply that any stumbling march towards death, interspersed with 'stations', is bound within our culture to suggest this parallel. But that does not make the parallel irrelevant; and the cumulative force of references individually disputable will surely lead us to conclude that a tentative identification of Johnny with Christ is more than a thing wished upon the film by over-zealous commentators. To posit some cunning allegory would seem inappropriate to this disjunctive text. Assuredly Johnny brings no redemption. If he bears some burden on behalf of all of us, then what manner of burden might that be?

A clue may be offered by words which follow closely upon one of the verses quoted by Johnny from Corinthians: '. . . now I know in part; but then shall I know even as also I am known.' It seems to me that the antithesis between knowing and being known, characterised by St Paul as a limitation of the earthly realm, lies at the heart of much that is distinctive in the filmic handling of *Odd Man Out*.

When we consider Johnny as the object of knowledge – whether our knowledge or that of the film's other characters – the sense of *objecthood* takes on a particular intensity. It is not simply that people speak of him as if he were a thing to be owned or given, wanted or sold; or that he is heaved and dumped as if he were a coal-sack. When he walks, the camerawork is of a style familiarly used to dehumanise Frankenstein's monster: he lurches away from us, knocking things down, or he is held in a backward tracking movement which denies us his viewpoint and hence his human purpose. His progress is accentuated by the 'fate' theme; and in contrast to normal practice, where film music is written to precise timings at the fine-cut stage, this was recorded in advance of the shooting, so that Mason could pace himself to its beat. Thus Johnny is made in quite a special sense subservient to the film's mechanism. He loses two hats in the course of the narrative: one, his disguise as a businessman, as he falls from the getaway car; the other, the flat cap which has been placed on his head as his coat is hung over his shoulders from behind, in the mud of the builder's yard. His holster and gun, tokens of the Organisation, are respectively discarded in the shelter and slipped down a drain. His sleeve is slit by the amateur first-aider; and the bandage unravels as if he were an exhumed and wandering mummy. If he is made to carry the meanings of others, these meanings seem unable to keep any purchase upon him.

Turning to the subjective aspect, we see that the major occasions when we are invited to share Johnny's consciousness are all marked by photographic trickery: the loss of focus on the steps of the mill; the mixing-on of prison bars, and of the little girl transformed into a hallucinatory warder, in the air-raid shelter; the appearance of talking faces in the beer bubbles; the marshalling of Lukey's paintings, and of the faint figure of Father Tom, in the studio scene. It may be objected that this is no more than a consequence of the story-line, which deals with a man in a state of delirium. But this delirium is not something which has a prior existence and simply awaits the choice of means for its expression. The 'delirium' is neither more nor less than the mode of knowledge constructed for us, through the operation of these cinematic devices, as Johnny's: the displacement of narrative elements, the superimposition (literally, optically) of one experience upon another – subjectivity as a hermetic recycling of data or, as in the case of the circling camera-movements and occasional soft focus on Johnny himself, the feedback of his supposed perception into our perception of him.

There is, then, an extreme differentiation between objective and subjective in the representation of Johnny; and this is reflected in a lack of reciprocity with other characters as expressed in the use of complementary camera set-ups. This is a difficult point to demonstrate, since it is a question of degree; but there is no doubt that the etiquettes of eyeline-matching are subtly and increasingly evaded. The tentatively cross-matched scenes with Dennis and with the young lovers in the air-raid shelter are disrupted by repeated loss of eye contact and by the guttering out of lights. In the scene with Rosie and Maudie, as I have remarked, the avoidance of exchanged looks becomes positively oppressive; and when Lukey is painting, we get no shot of Johnny from his point of view. The episodes with the cabby, with Shell and with Kathleen after their reunion are for the most part held in two-shot – the alternation of shots at the moment when Johnny and Kathleen meet serving only to register a brief last flicker of hope. All this contrasts sharply with the liberal use of cross-matching between other characters, between Johnny and others before the killing and – most significantly – between Johnny and his apparitions. The sense conveyed, that Johnny is part of another film, shot in a different idiom, induces a queasiness that is not Johnny's but ours. In narrative terms, the social mesh is torn by Johnny's being unable to reciprocate the attentions of others, and by their treatment of him as objective or instrumental. But it is the severance of *filmic* integration with the other characters that casts them as cameos and tinges them with absurdity.

Perhaps the most striking fact, in this connection, is that when Lukey gazes frustratedly at the painting in which he has hoped to capture 'that peculiar light in the eyes of a dying man', and then throws it down in dissatisfaction, we ourselves are not allowed to see it. Indeed, except for a few blurred frames as the easel falls at Johnny's departure, we do not see it at all. (Yet we know from the Two Cities advance publicity that such a painting was made – and was done in daily stages, so that its progress would be evident throughout the sequence.[16]) If this were a documentary, the withholding of our view of the painting would be intolerable; but here, we are being reminded, the inclusion of an unsatisfactory painting would be a filmic device of no greater inherent meaning than the actor's grimace at the evidence of his failure.

All fiction is a species of ontological polemic. The painting never existed beyond what we see of it – mainly the back of the canvas. Neither does Johnny exist beyond the way his representations mesh with others in the film. Of course, we may concede that no fictional character 'exists' in the sense in which characters in documentary precede their representations. What is special about Johnny is the way he forces this recognition to the point of crisis. To have shown us the painting would have undercut the camera's sustained distancing of Johnny by showing him refracted through the interpretative gaze of another; and we would have been constrained to 'take a view' ourselves on the question of its adequacy. (Interestingly, the lighting of Mason throughout the film has been so varied as to render him at moments – for example, with Dennis in the shelter – almost unrecognisable even to us as viewers.) But still, denial to us of an image which the story tells us *has* been painted marks a collapsing of narrational and narrated events. That is to say, Johnny's inaccessibility to others is being dramatised as an inaccessibility to us: dramatised through his non-existence outside the film's universe. It is the most severe, and arguably self-defeating, term in the process of his objectivisation.

At the same time there is a converse sense in which Johnny's subjectivity, through another collapsing of the narration and the narrated, begins itself to pervade this universe. Twice we have seen children enacting the incident on the steps of the mill – 'I'm Johnny McQueen!' – and once, two men dead on the steps of Theresa's house. Were it not for the fact that Johnny does not witness these things, and that in the former case there is a realistic 'explanation' (Johnny is passing into legend), these displacements of narrative content might more obviously reveal their kinship with those displacements we assign to his delirium. Again, not only Johnny but pairs of patrolling policemen, glimpsed briefly down side-streets, fall into pace with his music as if assimilated into his martyrdom – or, conversely, as if the elements of his make-up were being dismantled and stirred back into a primal lexicon of signs analogous to that proto-consciousness of which the city's children are its dispersed tatters. And there are other, odder instances. Before setting off for the robbery, Johnny breaks a shoelace; in the lead-up to the final scene, Shell breaks a shoelace. While Johnny is seeing faces in bubbles, Lukey is seeing faces in the fire. A shot of Shell confused by traffic at the crossroads – a quite complicated shot for which there is no narrative necessity – recalls the earlier incident where Johnny in his confusion was nearly knocked down by a lorry; and the very gratuitousness of this shot may prompt us to read new significance into Dennis's foreshadowing of Johnny's bandaged arm, or the little girl's fleeting resemblance to him. Furthermore Shell, who carries the main weight of these displacements, is a character who habitually talks in substitutions – a budgerigar for the fugitive – and whose very name suggests an empty receptacle.

Thus if the 'Frankenstein' objectivity and the subjectivity of delirium are polarised and irreconcilable, the two behave differently when brought up against the limits of narration: the former ending in absence (that of the painted image); the latter sustaining a phantom life, distributed into the representation of others, so that even as subjectivity it is unsettled. What *Odd Man Out* does is to make the disintegrating consciousness of the condemned man, his inability to reconcile knowing and being known, into its structuring principle: so that in construing the film's grammars we endorse it. The objective and the subjective stories are alike shown as untellable.

....

Earlier I left unanswered the question whether a certain resemblance to *L'Étranger* should be considered superficial or profound. It is difficult to see in the extremity of Johnny's situation, and in the way he is represented as virtually unrepresentable, a simple parallel with the 'philosophical autism' which I suggested was embodied in Meursault. Johnny is almost the antithesis of the existential hero, in that his progress is inexorably towards that state – which is death – of existing solely for others. But it does seem to me that such autism is displayed, if not by Johnny towards his world, then by his world towards him: imprisoning his subjectivity by a lack of true responses. This is revealed in another aspect of the film's construction. Normally, when complementary shots are cut against each other in a dialogue scene, there is a certain amount of overlapping of one person's speech into shots of the other listening and reacting: a device designed not only to affirm human interactivity but to knit the two images together into one suppositional space. In *Odd Man Out* this is scarcely ever done. (Indeed, much of the emotional power of Johnny's cry of anguish in the pub derives from the fact that it does, exceptionally, occur entirely over shots of other people.) The effect of this forswearing of customary practice is not only to emphasise the separateness of individuals but to risk a disintegration of the film's spatial construction in a way that can at times – particularly in the studio sequences – become positively disturbing: each character not only isolated, but carrying a fragment of narrative space into that isolation.

Odd Man Out maintains an abrasive relationship with its aesthetic resources; and, like other works of which this may be said – the figures of Giacometti, perhaps, or some of the late piano writing of Liszt – it gains a distinctive fascination from that. The abrasiveness, the putting under stress of its own means and its own materials, in this case is manifest at many levels, from the insistence upon heterogeneity at the possible expense of stylistic coherence to the willingness to push representation to the point of its own breakdown. The fascination of the 'abrasive' work resides in its making explicit the ultimatum with which all art in one way or another confronts us: To find meaning in this is to accede to its polemic, to declare yourself for the proposition that its language constitutes a legitimate articulation of the human state. What, then, is being articulated by the radical separation of the subjective and objective components of a human identity? It is the vision of a person stripped of those reciprocities, socially given or individually chosen, within which the two might live comfortably together: of a world where all contacts have become attenuated or meretricious or debased. But it is also the recognition, with St Paul, that knowledge and being known are ultimately irreconcilable for all of us.

The recklessness with which the film beats against its own expressive limits, as if against the bars of a cage, challenges us to accept that these are the limits of experience and of our humanity; and, to the extent that we acknowledge this vision, the film's plea for charity is raised above – far above, in my view – the hollow pietism that its religiose setting might suggest. If I elect to speak of *Odd Man Out* in terms of metaphysical rebellion, rather than of the defeatism which Anstey implied in his association of it with the German cinema of the 1920s, it is, I think, solely because of the exhilaration inseparable from that challenge. In which case perhaps Johnny is, as Camus was finally to say of Meursault, the only Christ we deserve.[17]

AFTERWORD
. . . .

Frederick Laurence Green, born in Portsmouth in 1902, had settled in Belfast in 1932. Of his fourteen or so novels, one – *On the Night of the*

Fire – had already been filmed in 1939 by Brian Desmond Hurst. Carol Reed would certainly have known about this, since his wife, Diana Wynyard, had taken the leading female role.

Reed saw the job of a director as 'to convey faithfully what the author had in mind';[18] and he persuaded Green, despite the latter's doubts about his capabilities as a screen writer, to collaborate on the adaptation of *Odd Man Out*. Yet the tone of the book is so different from that of the film, especially in its earlier passages, that it comes as something of a surprise to find whole chunks of the dialogue transferred unaltered; and one begins to wonder whether Reed's motive in involving the writer was not – as with the mingling of diverse acting styles – more to do with maintaining the breadth of his trawl. To put it crudely, Reed seems to hate no one, whereas Green seems to hate practically everyone.[19] But some of the subtler differences are more interesting.

The book of *Odd Man Out* is narrated in the third person: not a third person designed to simulate the objective gaze, but rather that variety in which the author feels free to dip at will into the subjective

Joseph Tomelty (l.) with Carol Reed

feelings of any character. (If such a treatment commonly attracts the designation 'realism', this can be only in some quasi-Platonic sense whereby inferential forms are granted reality, for it has no equivalent at all in human experience.) It opens with a description of the mill towering over the deserted street, and of the arrival of the car at its entrance. Then, at the end of the third paragraph, as the three men climb the steps, it tells us of their cheerful conversation 'ending abruptly when the heavy door swung to behind them'. At this moment the narration, without ceasing to be in all essentials third-person, has become spatially situated in the scene: as occupying a position from which the men's speech has ceased to be audible. Such, of course, is the condition of all film narrative, in that every scene must be viewed *from* somewhere; and we may fantasise this as the point in his reading of the novel when Reed began seeing it as a potential movie.

Although every film image implies a camera position, it has not been found convenient to organise narrative in cinema by identifying camera positions with those occupied by characters. (Everyone would end up looking straight out of the screen at us, and space would tend always to become locked onto an axis between two people.) The preferred solution, particularly in Anglo-American cinema, has been to

(l. to r.) Unknown technician, Carol Reed, Robert Krasker, Laurie Friedman construct, from the cross-matching of eyelines a few degrees removed from that of the camera, a sort of non-Euclidean space in which the positions occupied by the camera are felt not to exist. By this means, a third-person, 'objective' narration can be conjured out of the acknowledgment of space as being defined by the viewpoints of individuals. (Except for one or two unmemorable 'subjective camera' experiments, a true first-person narration occurs in cinema only in documentary, which – at least in its more *vérité* manifestations – is saying to us, 'This is what I, the camera, have seen.')

It is this set of visual conventions, matured over the previous three decades, that the film of *Odd Man Out* handles so roughly in striving to represent Johnny's condition. In the book, his isolation is actually more extreme, his pain and delirium more unrelieved – and in that, perhaps, more realistically rendered, though by the same token less able to serve as a metaphor for our everyday lives. While he can just about summon the energy to smear Lukey's portrait of him, the Johnny of the book could never have risen to declaim the passage from Corinthians. To an extent, Green's willingness to enter the subjectivity of all his characters has robbed him of the opportunity to set the extreme subjectivity of Johnny's delirium starkly against his bodily presence in the world of others. It would undoubtedly have been a more powerful piece of work. But we cannot help being struck by the fact that, in the film, it is the fundamental premises of the medium's expressivity which are being challenged in the attempt to portray a man for whom knowing and being known – seeing and being seen, occupying space and generating space – have become dislocated.

I noted at the outset that the death of a central character in a film leaves it bereft not only of an object of scrutiny and contemplation but of a generative principle. By leaving the very *space* impoverished, it takes on a special sorrow. It seems to me likewise that the differences between the film and the book of *Odd Man Out* – the ones that matter most – depend less from differences in outlook between Green and Reed than from the contrasting limitations and potentialities of film and literature. Anyone who supposes that literature has no blind areas might care to ask why, in the book, the seeing or not-seeing of Lukey's portrait of Johnny does not arise as an issue.

. . . .

Because the book's dialogue has largely been scissors-and-pasted into the film, rather than being rewritten to suit the altered emphases and lengths and structuring of the episodes, there are occasions when the book seems to offer help towards the film's elucidation. It is clear, for example, that in the book the word 'faith' is accorded a special meaning: something akin to 'courage', or even 'life-affirmation'. But we must, I think, refuse such help if we are to respond to the film as a work in its own right, not least because such reliance upon the source might blind us to the wealth of interpretative options which the film offers and the book does not. Indeed, I wonder whether it has been obvious how far my problem in this enterprise has been one of deciding where to call a halt. When remarking upon the resemblance of Lukey and Tober to adoring saints in a religious tableau, would it have been pertinent to mention the tradition whereby St Luke was a painter and had executed a portrait of the Virgin Mary? (Consider the difference it would have made to our iconographic heritage if an authenticated likeness of the Virgin Mary had survived to our time; and then ask whether this has any bearing upon the denial to us of Lukey's portrait of Johnny.)

Or let us take a less recondite example: the two boys who open the curtain and shed a potentially revealing light on Johnny. They peer upwards, as if identifying a constellation. Yet what can they possibly be looking at through such a blizzard? Perhaps it is the clock – which, after all, has been visible through almost all windows – but we are given no reason to assume this. Some commentators have described them as watching the snow falling, but their combined gaze seems too focused for that. We may simply shrug and decide that Reed was being a little careless with this shot. And yet, the moment we do so, we are struck again by the strange *rightness* of it. Does it come down to the fact that the boys are not looking at Johnny: that their preoccupations are already excluding him while their actions still put him in danger? Maybe. But is there not also something haunted in the very conception of these boys looking towards where nothing may be seen? And again one pauses and asks: am I not overloading this simple image with implications?

I do not believe this is a difficulty that would have presented itself with any and every film I might have chosen to write about. There is a sense in which *Odd Man Out* seems to bleed into the world, perhaps because it represents the point of intersection of many cultural forces.

We have already discussed the contributions of the US censor, of the wartime taste for the supernatural, of the postwar vogue for child-centred tales. Even mysterious policemen seem to have been a part of the *Zeitgeist*: J. B. Priestley's *An Inspector Calls* had opened in 1946. And those critics who have noted the influence of the prewar work of Carné and Prévert have failed to mention that 1939 saw the release of a minor film, co-scripted (and possibly co-directed) by James Mason, which starred himself as a murderer on the run given shelter by a woman who has the ulterior motive of wishing to write about him; and that this film, too, was edited by Fergus McDonell.[20]

The makers of *Odd Man Out* cannot have known that the winter of 1946–7 would prove one of the worst in memory. Yet their work seems to settle into its historical context as if by right: as if it were almost a phenomenon of nature, or at any rate a product of both human and less ponderable forces. When I step back from it, what I see is a great Piranesian monument built from the detritus of former monuments, or a Vanbrugh palace whose passageways are inexhaustible and whose echoes return in the stillness when we think they have died.

The two boys looking up through the window

NOTES

....

1 Albert Camus, *The Rebel* (translation by Anthony Bower of *L'Homme révolté*, 1951), with foreword by Herbert Read (Harmondsworth: Peregrine, 1962), p. 30 and p. 7.

2 James Mason, *Before I Forget* (London: Hamish Hamilton, 1981), pp. 255–6.

3 Columbia News Service, quoted in *Guardian*, 2 August 1962.

4 F. L. Green, *Odd Man Out* (London: Michael Joseph, 1945). For the 1991 Cardinal Books paperback, it has still evidently been considered a selling-point to have a publicity photograph from the film on the cover.

5 Albert Camus, *L'Étranger* (1942), published in English as *The Outsider* (Harmondsworth: Penguin, 1983), pp. 58–60.

6 A thorough account of Asperger's syndrome is provided by Oliver Sacks in 'An Anthropologist on Mars', *New Yorker*, 27 December 1993, pp. 106–25.

7 The sequence of the raid and the getaway is analysed in detail, and with special attention to the expressive use of ostensibly natural sound, in Karel Reisz, *The Technique of Film Editing* (London and New York: Focal Press, 1953), pp. 260–70.

8 James de Felice, *Filmguide to Odd Man Out* (Bloomington: Indiana University Press, 1975).

9 I am indebted here to Gabriel Josipovici's *The Book of God* (New Haven and London: Yale University Press, 1988), where accounts of this incident in the Gospels of Matthew, Mark and Luke are compared (pp. 217–18).

10 The pre-production script was published in Roger Manvell (ed.), *Three British Screenplays* (London: Methuen, 1950). It differs in several major respects, including the names of some characters, from the finished film.

11 Reg Whiteley, *Daily Mirror*, 31 May 1946.

12 Harold Pinter, *Old Times* (London: Faber & Faber, 1971). An account of an encounter in a fleapit where *Odd Man Out* is showing, and of a shared passion for the persona of Robert Newton, provides one point of focus amid a shimmer of overlapping memories perhaps true, perhaps false.

13 Mason, *Before I Forget*, p. 163.

14 Carol Reed quoted by Nicholas Wapshott in *The Man Between* (London: Chatto & Windus, 1990), p. 186. (Regrettably, Wapshott gives no sources.) A conspiracy theory of the time held that the US censors were deliberately emasculating British films in order to scupper the competition. This was given voice in a parody of *Jabberwocky* by I. A. L. Diamond, which appeared in the American *The Screen Writer* in 1947 and was reprinted in *Documentary Newsletter*. One stanza must suffice:

> And as in quota-quotes he stood,
> The Jarthurank, of happy breed,
> Came boulting through the korda wood
> And carolled on his reed.

15 A similar gesture, so far as I can tell in reproduction, occurs in the *Last Judgment* of Fra Bartolommeo, in the Museo di San Marco, Florence.

16 Two Cities Films Ltd, *Bulletin*, 3 June 1946.

17 Camus, 8 January 1955. Included as Afterword in the Penguin edition of *The Outsider*, pp. 118–19.

18 Reed interviewed by W. J. Weatherby in the *Guardian*, 26 November 1959.

19 In the book, Johnny's surname is Murtah, easily misheard as 'murder'. In the film it is McQueen, with its princely connotations.

20 *I Met a Murderer* is billed as having been directed by Roy Kellino, but Mason writes as if Kellino had been only the cameraman (*Before I Forget*, p. 163).

CREDITS

· ·

Odd Man Out

UK
1947
Production company
Two Cities Films
UK trade show
29 January 1947
UK release
17 March 1947
Distributor (UK)
General Film Distributors
In charge of production
F. Del Giudice
Producer/director
Carol Reed
Associate producer
Phil C. Samuel
Production manager
Frank Bevis
Assistant director
Mark Evans
Second assistant director
Tony Hearne
Screenplay
F. L. Green, R. C. Sherriff
from the novel by
F. L. Green
Photography (black and white)
Robert Krasker
Camera operator
Russell Thomson,
Laurie Friedman
Stills
Dave Bolton
Music
William Alwyn
Music played by
London Symphony
Orchestra conducted by
Muir Mathieson
Editor
Fergus McDonell
Assistant editor
Geoffrey Muller
Production decor
Roger Furse

Art director
Ralph Brinton
Wardrobe buyer
Peggy Henderson
Make-up
H. Hutchinson
Special effects
Stanley Grant, Bill
Warrington
Sound editor
Harry Miller
Sound recordists
A. Fisher, Desmond Dew
Backings
E. Lindegaard
Continuity
Olga Brooks
Irish advisers
Cecil Ford, Joseph Tomelty
116 minutes

James Mason
Johnny McQueen
Robert Newton
Lukey
Cyril Cusack
Pat
F. J. McCormick
Shell
William Hartnell
Fencie, the barman
Fay Compton
Rosie
Denis O'Dea
Inspector
W. G. Fay
Father Tom
Elwyn Brook Jones
Tober
Robert Beatty
Dennis
Dan O'Herlihy
Nolan
Kitty Kirwan
Granny
Beryl Measor
Maudie
Roy Irving
Murphy

Joseph Tomelty
'Gin' Jimmy, the cabbie
Arthur Hambling
Tom
Ann Cleary
Maureen
Eddie Byrne
Seaman
Maureen Delaney
Theresa O'Brien
Kathleen Ryan
Kathleen Sullivan
Noel Purcell
Tram conductor
Guy Rolfe
Policeman searching Kathleen's house
Min Milligan
Father Tom's housekeeper
Dora Bryan
Girl in telephone kiosk
Geoffery Keen
Soldier
Maura Milligan
Maureen Cusack

Odd Man Out was remade
by Universal in 1969 as
The Lost Man, produced by
Edward Muhl, directed by
Robert Alan Aurthur and
starring Sidney Poitier and
Joanna Shimkus. It was set
against a background of the
US civil rights movement.

Credits checked by Markku
Salmi. The print of *Odd Man
Out* in the National Film and
Television Archive derives
from material deposited by
the Rank Organisation in
1955.

BIBLIOGRAPHY

· ·

1. Books

Armes, Roy. *A Critical History of the British Cinema* (London: Secker & Warburg, 1978).

De Felice, James. *Filmguide to Odd Man Out* (Bloomington: Indiana University Press, 1975).

Durgnat, Raymond. *A Mirror for England* (London: Faber & Faber, 1970).

Green, F. L. *Odd Man Out* (London: Sphere, 1991).

Manvell, Roger (ed.). *Three British Screenplays* (London: Methuen, 1950).

Mason, James. *Before I Forget* (London: Hamish Hamilton, 1981).

Moss, Robert F. *The Films of Carol Reed* (London: Macmillan, 1987).

Murphy, Robert, *Realism and Tinsel – Cinema and Society in Britain 1939–49* (London: Routledge, 1989).

Reisz, Karel. *The Technique of Film Editing* (London and New York: Focal Press, 1953).

Wapshott, Nicholas. *The Man Between* (London: Chatto & Windus, 1990).

2. Articles

Anstey, Edgar and Wright, Basil. *Documentary News Letter*, April/May 1947.

Sarris, Andrew. 'First of the Realists', *Films and Filming*, September 1957, and 'The Stylist Goes to Hollywood', *Films and Filming*, October 1957.

Sulka, Walter. *Documentary News Letter*, June/July 1947.

Vesselo, Arthur. 'Films of the Quarter', *Sight and Sound*, Summer 1947.

Yerrill, D. A. 'The Still, Small Voice', *Sight and Sound*, Autumn 1947.

ALSO PUBLISHED

If you would like further information about future BFI Film Classics or about other books on film, media and popular culture from BFI Publishing, please write to:

**BFI Film Classics
British Film Institute
21 Stephen Street
London
W1P 2LN**